Eh, Canada?
Familiar Phrases

Pocket-Sized

Canadian Trivia

Books

I0092638

Written an...
Illustrated by
Jacqueline Cooper

Large Print Edition

Published by Little Goodbyes Press

www.littlegoodbyes.ca

Large Print Edition
Set in Lexend 16 pt type

Publisher's Cataloguing-in-
Publication data

Familiar Phrases / Jacqueline
Cooper.

ISBN 978-1-997874-18-8

1. Canada—Miscellanea.

2. Curiosities and wonders—
Canada. 3. Saying— Canada—
Humour.

I. Title.

About the Series

Eh, Canada? is a series of tiny books stuffed with big trivia. Each volume dives into the quirky, peculiar, and sometimes downright ridiculous sides of Canadian life including outdated laws, incredible inventions, odd foods to strange animals, haunted places, and more.

They're pocket-sized, easy to flip through, and perfect for stocking stuffers, coffee tables, or anywhere you need a dose of, "Wait, is that really true?"

Because let's face it: Canada is polite, proud, and just a little bit absurd. And that's exactly why we love it.

Table of Contents

Said in Canada

Canada is known for snowstorms, strong coffee, and apologizing even when nothing is our fault.

Our language has its own personality too, with regional quirks, cottage-country slang, and everyday words that make sense here and nowhere else.

This book celebrates

the way Canadians talk, from phrases you hear coast to coast to the expressions that only appear once you cross a certain provincial line. Some entries are practical, others are funny, and a few are so normal to us that we forget they sound unusual anywhere else.

So grab a regular coffee, get comfortable, and enjoy a look at the small everyday expressions that help shape life in Canada, one word at a time.

Classic Canadiana

Eh?

Meaning: A friendly tag that turns a statement into a question or a gentle check-in.

Common where: Across Canada, especially in Ontario and the Prairies.

First heard: In the early 1800s letters and stories from settlers who already sounded a bit Canadian.

The story: Linguists call it a "tag particle," but Canadians just use it to keep things polite. Add eh? to almost anything and suddenly you're part of the conversation.

Double-Double

Meaning: Coffee with two creams and two sugars.

Common where: Across Canada

First recorded: Late 20th century, spread through everyday use.

The story: The phrase never needed advertising in Canada or a trademark as it naturally spread through drive-thru windows and morning chatter. Order one anywhere else and you'll probably have to explain yourself, which only makes Canadians more loyal to it.

The phrase is so ingrained in the culture that it was added to the Canadian Oxford Dictionary in 2004, though the actual trademark belongs to In-N-Out Burger in the U.S.

Canuck

Meaning: A nickname for a Canadian.

Common where: Everywhere in Canada, and by hockey fans around the world thanks to the Vancouver Canucks.

First heard: Early 1800s. The word likely came from the Hawaiian kanaka ("person"), used by sailors to describe Polynesian workers. Early American writers used it to not so politely describe French Canadians. Over time it spread to mean any Canadian.

The story: Once mildly mocking, it's now worn with pride on jerseys, t-shirts, and the occasional tattoo. Only in Canada could an old insult turn into a team mascot.

Pop

Meaning: The Canadian word for a carbonated soft drink or what most of the world calls soda.

Common where: Across most of Canada, especially the Prairies and central provinces.

First heard: In 1812 the poet Robert Southey wrote in a letter of 'a new manufactory of a nectar, between soda-water and ginger-beer, and called pop.' Eventually these drinks became known as soda pop. After that is where the invisible line was drawn between the U.S. and Canada, Canadians picked pop and Americans shifted to soda.

The story: The name may come from the sound, but Canadians kept it for the taste, just ask anyone who's ever ordered a "diet pop" and gotten a funny look abroad.

Hydro

Meaning: Canadian shorthand for electricity or the

electric utility company, as in "I need to pay my hydro bill."

Common where: Across Canada especially British Columbia, Ontario and Quebec.

First heard: Early 1900s, when many provinces established publicly owned hydroelectric power companies.

Hydroelectric power is electricity generated from the power of moving water, typically through dams. The nickname stuck even after other power sources joined the grid.

The story: Elsewhere, "hydro" means water. In Canada, it means the lights, the fridge, and the thing you panic about when the bill arrives.

Serviette

Meaning: The Canadian word for a paper napkin, you know the thing you grab when the poutine betrays you. Napkin is the general term for both paper and cloth varieties.

Common where: Across Canada.

First heard: Borrowed directly from French in the 1400s, but kept alive in Canada through everyday bilingual influence. It appears in Canadian English writing from the early 1900s onward.

The story:
Everywhere else, serviette sounds a bit fancy. In Canada, it's just regular Tuesday

dinner table vocabulary and another reminder what happens when two languages share one table.

Runners

Meaning: Everyday Canadian word for athletic shoes or sneakers.

Common where: Widely used across Canada, especially in

schools and casual conversation.

First heard: Dates back to early-20th-century running shoes; Canadians simply shortened the phrase and never looked back.

The story: Whether you're dashing to catch the bus or just running errands, runners are what you wear, even if actual

running is the last
thing on your mind.

Pencil Crayons

Meaning: The
colourful drawing
tools Canadians of all
ages reach for known
elsewhere as coloured
pencils.

Common where:
Common across
English-speaking
Canada, especially in
schools and art

supplies lists.

First heard: Appears in Canadian school vocabulary from the mid-1900s, likely influenced by crayon de couleur from French.

The story: A straightforward name that does what it says: a pencil that's also a crayon. Simple, practical, and perfectly Canadian.

Chesterfield

Meaning: A sofa or couch (you know the kind your grandparents wouldn't let you eat on), sometimes covered in doilies.

Common where: Once heard across Canada, especially in Ontario and the Prairies; still used by older generations and in smaller towns.

First heard: The word comes from a British furniture style popular in the 1800s, but Canadians held onto it long after others switched to sofa or couch.

The story: A word that sounds fancy but really just means "the big seat in the living room." Even if fewer people say it now,

every Canadian
knows exactly what it
means.

Cold Talk

Chinook

Meaning: A warm, dry wind that blows down the eastern slopes of the Rockies, turning winter back into spring for a few fleeting days.

Common where: Western Canada, especially southern Alberta. Calgary is famous for its sudden Chinooks.

First heard: The word originally referred to the Chinook people. When settlers encountered warm, dry winds blowing in from the Pacific and adopted the name of the local tribes to describe the phenomenon. They also called the winds "snow eaters" because they could melt snow quickly but for some reason that name didn't stick.

The story: When temperatures jump from –25°C to +10°C overnight, you don't ask questions. You just enjoy it, then pretend to be surprised when winter returns two days later.

Tuque

(Toque/Touque)

Meaning: A knitted winter hat that's cuffed, cozy, and completely Canadian with the occasional pom-pom.

Common where: Nationwide.

First heard: From the French word tuque, which originally meant any kind of hat, including the chef's tall white version. Canadians simply kept the word and stuffed it with wool instead. Its Canadian winter meaning dates to the 1800s, when voyageurs and loggers wore them through brutal cold.

The story: Globally, a tuque blanche

belongs in a kitchen; here, it's what you grab before scraping frost off your windshield because when your eyelashes freeze, you deserve your own word for headgear.

Winterpeg

Meaning: A nickname for Winnipeg, Manitoba that's half joke, half weather report.

Common where:
Used across Canada, often by Winnipeggers themselves with a mix of pride and frostbite.

First heard:
Appeared in print by the mid-1900s as a playful twist on the city's name, thanks to its reputation for long, brutal winters. And since the early 2000s

the nickname is now directly associated with positive, uniquely Winnipeg winter experiences, such as the Nestaweya River Trail at The Forks.

The story: When the temperature hits –40°C and you still go to work, you earn the right to rename your city. Winterpeg might sound teasing, but it's mostly a badge of endurance.

Ice Road

Meaning: A temporary winter road built over frozen lakes and tundra.

Common where: Northern Canada, from Manitoba to the Arctic.

First heard: Mid-1900s, when engineers began

constructing winter supply routes for isolated communities and mines.

The story: Every year, Canada builds about 10,000 kms of these icy highways, linking places the rest of the world only reaches by plane. Other cold countries make them too, but nowhere relies on them quite like Canada, where

they appear each
winter and vanish
with the thaw.

Snowbird

Meaning: A Canadian
who escapes winter
by heading south for
the season often to
Florida, Arizona, or
Mexico.

Common where:
Across Canada,
especially among
retirees and RV

travelers.

First heard:
Mid-1900s, when post-war prosperity made winter migration possible for more Canadians.

The story: Named after the birds that actually migrate, snowbirds follow the sun instead of the flock. They trade parkas for palm trees every year, proving

that sometimes
survival means just
booking a flight.

Hydro Outage

Meaning: A power
failure when the lights
suddenly go out, the
house goes quiet, and
everyone reaches for
a flashlight.

Common where:
Across Canada,
especially in winter
when ice, wind, or

heavy snow bring down the lines.

First heard: Mid-1900s, after provinces created their public Hydro utilities. Canadians soon shortened "hydroelectric outage" to "hydro outage," and the phrase stuck.

The story: It's the only time Canadians truly test their

emergency kits and
their patience.

When the hydro's out,
the furnace is off, the
Wi-Fi is gone, and
conversation makes a
brief comeback.

Polite Talk (That Isn't Always Polite)

Sorry

Meaning: A word that Canadians use to apologize, sympathize, ask a question, or just politely acknowledge someone's existence.

Common where: Everywhere in Canada. Heard in doorways, grocery aisles, and any situation where two people try to move in the same direction.

First heard: From the Old English sārig ("sorrowful"), but Canada turned it into a reflex.

The country even passed a 2009 "Apology Act" clarifying that saying "sorry" in court doesn't count as admitting guilt.

The story: Canadians

don't just say sorry when we've done something wrong, we say it when you have. It's less about guilt and more about keeping the peace.

Yeah, No, For Sure

Meaning: A friendly, low-pressure way of saying "yes." It's a polite contradiction that somehow agrees with everyone.

Common where: Across Canada, especially in casual chat and customer service.

First heard: For sure was recorded in North American English since the early 1500s, but Canadians perfected its calm, agreeable tone.

The story: Yeah, no,

for sure is the verbal equivalent of a warm nod, it's positive, polite, and just noncommittal enough to keep the peace.

No Worries

Meaning: A friendly way to say "it's fine" or "don't mention it." It often replaces "you're welcome" or smooths over small inconveniences.

Common where:
Heard everywhere in
Canada, from coffee
shops to customer
service counters.

First heard: Imported
from British and
Australian English in
the late 20th century,
but quickly adopted
into Canadian
politeness culture.

The story: Canadians
made it their own by
adding reassurance

to everything.
Whether you spilled a
drink, showed up late,
or thanked someone
twice, the answer's
the same: no worries.

That's

Interesting

Meaning: A polite
Canadian way of
responding when you
don't fully agree,
don't want to argue,

or aren't sure what to say next.

Common where:
Everywhere. It's used in conversations between friends, coworkers, and complete strangers who want to stay friendly.

First heard: The phrase itself is centuries old, but Canadians turned it into a soft landing in the mid-20th century, using tone rather than words to signal what they really mean.

The story: Depending on how it's said, it can mean "tell me more," "I'm not convinced," or "let's never revisit this topic again." Only Canadians could turn two harmless words into a full emotional spectrum.

Buddy / Guy

Meaning: Two casual ways to address someone and are friendly, teasing, or mildly annoyed, depending entirely on tone.

Common where: Heard across Canada in greetings, jokes, and moments when two people try to walk through the same doorway.

First heard: Both words have long histories in English, but Canadians turned them into tone-driven tools: "Hey buddy!" means you're welcome, and "Listen, buddy..." means you're not.

The story: In Canada, buddy can make someone feel included or gently warned. It all comes down to the delivery, which Canadians have perfected into an art form.

Beauty

Meaning: A warm, enthusiastic compliment used for anything impressive like a great idea, a perfect day, a lucky moment, or a well-timed joke.

Common where:
Heard across Canada,
especially in sports,
outdoorsy chatter,
and everyday praise.

First heard: Used
informally since the
early 1900s, when
Canadians began
turning simple
adjectives into
friendly exclamations.

The story: Whether
it's a smooth play on
the ice or the first

warm day in April, Canadians don't just say it's good, they say it's a beauty. It's praise delivered with a grin.

Keener

Meaning: Someone who's eager, prepared, or a little too enthusiastic you know the classmate who had their hand up before the question was even asked.

Common where: Used across Canada in classrooms, workplaces, and anywhere effort is easy to spot.

First heard: In Canadian English by the mid-1900s, built from the older word keen meaning eager or sharp. Canadians added "-er" and turned it into a personality.

The story: Elsewhere, keener simply means "more keen," and in older usage it can even refer to someone who laments at funerals. In Canada, it's a light, good-natured nudge toward the person who's just a bit more enthusiastic than everyone else.

Food & Drink

Butter Tart

Meaning: A small pastry with a gooey, buttery filling sometimes with raisins, sometimes very firmly without.

Common where: Found across Canada in bakeries, farmers' markets, cafés, and family recipe boxes.

First heard: Recipes appeared in Ontario

cookbooks in the early 1900s, likely inspired by older Scottish and French tarts, but the Canadian name and style quickly became distinct.

The story: Few foods spark stronger opinions than the great raisin debate. Whether you pick team with or without, butter tarts are a sweet piece of Canadiana in every bite.

Regular Coffee

Meaning: A standard coffee order meaning one cream and one sugar, no guessing, no customizing, just "regular."

Common where: Widely used across Canada at diners, drive-thrus, and coffee counters.

First heard: Became common in the mid-20th century when coffee orders were simpler and "regular" meant the most typical mix. Canadians kept the meaning long after cafés got complicated.

The story: Order a regular anywhere else in the world and you might get black coffee or a puzzled look. In Canada, it's the easiest order of the day with just one cream, one sugar, and zero explanation needed.

Caesar

Meaning: A savoury cocktail made with vodka, clam-tomato juice (Clamato), hot sauce, and

Worcestershire and usually served with celery, lime, or whatever creative garnish the bar dreams up.

Common where: Across Canada, from pubs to patios to brunch menus. It's far less known outside the country, where bartenders often mistake it for a Bloody Mary.

First heard: Invented in Calgary in 1969 by bartender Walter Chell, who was asked to create a signature drink for a new Italian restaurant. His clam-infused twist became an instant Canadian classic.

The story: Bold, briny, and endlessly customizable, the Caesar became Canada's go-to brunch drink. Whether garnished with pickles, pepperoni, or an entire slider, there's nothing more Canadian than ordering something the rest of the world doesn't even recognize.

Kraft Dinner (KD)

Meaning: Kraft boxed macaroni and cheese known in Canada almost exclusively as KD.

Common where: Everywhere. It's a pantry staple, student meal, and childhood classic across the country.

First heard: Sold in Canada since the 1930s, with the short form KD becoming widespread by the late 20th century. Canadians buy more of it per capita than anywhere else.

The story: In Canada it isn't mac and cheese, it's KD, a two-letter comfort food with decades of nostalgia packed into a bright blue box. It's safe to say this is Canada's unofficial dish.

Two-Four

Meaning: A case of 24 beers aka the classic long weekend supply.

Common where: Used across Canada, especially in Ontario and the Prairies, and tied closely to May 24th ("the May Two-

Four"), the unofficial start of summer.

First heard: Appeared in Canadian speech and advertising by the mid-1900s as beer packaging standardized into 24-bottle cases.

The story: Whether it's for a cottage trip, a backyard gathering, or a long weekend tradition, Canadians don't ask for a case of beer, they ask for a two-four. It's both a measurement and a mood.

BeaverTail

Meaning: A flat, hand-stretched piece of fried dough, often topped with cinnamon sugar, chocolate, or fruit.

Common where: Popular at winter

festivals, skating rinks, and tourist spots across Canada. These treats were first sold in Ontario and later spread nationwide.

First heard: The name appeared in the late 1970s when the family business that created the pastry began selling it at fairs. The long and flattened shape inspired the playful name.

The story: It's warm, sweet, and best eaten outdoors with cold fingers. Canadians may not agree on the best topping, but everyone agrees it's not truly winter without at least one BeaverTail.

Poutine

Meaning: A hearty

dish made of French fries, cheese curds, and hot gravy truly a comfort food with a cult following.

Common where: Most strongly associated with Quebec, but now served across Canada in diners, pubs, food trucks, and late-night spots.

First heard: Created in rural Quebec in the late 1950s, when cheese curds were added to fries and gravy at small snack bars. The name's origin is debated, but early stories link it to a slang word meaning "mess."

The story: What started as a simple roadside meal became a national favourite. The secret is in the fresh squeaky curds and in accepting that some things taste better if they're a little messy.

Mickey

Meaning: A small bottle of liquor, usually around 375 ml which is just big enough to fit in a coat pocket.

Common where: Widely used in Canadian conversation and

liquor stores; the term isn't common outside Canada.

First heard: In use by the early 20th century, likely derived from older slang for small flasks or discreet bottles.

The story: A mickey is the perfect size for bringing along something to drink. Its name is so familiar that many Canadians don't realize it's a regional term until they travel and ask for one elsewhere.

Nanaimo Bar

Meaning: A no-bake dessert with a crumbly base, custard-flavoured middle, and a thin chocolate top layer.

Common where: Across Canada, with the strongest roots on Vancouver Island, particularly in the city of Nanaimo.

First heard: Recipes circulated by the mid-20th century, especially in B.C. community cookbooks. The name solidified as the bar gained popularity nationwide.

The story: Simple, rich, and instantly recognizable, the Nanaimo bar became a Canadian favourite long before regional pride turned it into a culinary icon. It's the kind of dessert everyone claims their family has "the" best version of.

Everyday Life

Loonie

Meaning: Canada's one-dollar coin, named for the loon that appears on one side.

Common where: Everywhere. It's the everyday coin in pockets, parking meters, and vending machines.

First heard: Introduced in 1987

when Canada replaced the one-dollar bill with a gold-coloured coin. The nickname loonie appeared almost immediately in newspapers and stuck within weeks.

The story: Outside Canada, "loony" usually just means eccentric and talking about it will get you funny looks. It's safe to say Canadians didn't just accept the coin, they made it iconic.

It's the only currency where a national bird quietly became the unofficial name for a whole denomination.

Toonie

Meaning: Canada's two-dollar coin, it's a bi-metal coin with the polar bear in the centre.

Common where:
Used everywhere in Canada alongside the loonie; it quickly became part of everyday speech and spending.

First heard:
Introduced in 1996 to replace the two-dollar bill. The nickname toonie emerged within days as a natural partner to

loonie, and newspapers adopted it almost immediately.

The story: The name wasn't officially chosen by the Mint, Canadians came up with it on their own. Outside Canada, it sounds like cartoon money, but here it's just what you call two bucks in coin form.

Garburator

Meaning: A kitchen sink grinder that chews up food scraps before they go down the drain.

Common where: Used across Canada in home listings, kitchen renovations, and everyday conversation.

First heard: It appeared in Canadian

English by the mid-20th century, formed from garbage and the "-ator" ending is from carburetor.

The story: In most places it's a disposal. In Canada it's a garburator, a word so common in housing ads and home inspections that Canadians are often surprised to learn it's not used anywhere else.

Muskoka Chair

Meaning: The classic wooden outdoor chair with wide arms and a slanted back that's perfect for cottage decks and lakeside docks.

Common where: Most widely used in Ontario, especially in cottage country

around Muskoka.
Elsewhere it's more
often called an
Adirondack chair.

First heard: Gained
popularity in the
mid-20th century as
tourism and cottaging
expanded in the
Muskoka region. The
name stuck locally
and became part of
Ontario summer
vocabulary.

The story: Whatever you call it, Canadians know the chair: heavy, wooden, and impossible to move quietly. In Muskoka, though, it's not an Adirondack, it's a Muskoka chair, and summer doesn't start until you sit in one.

Give'r

Meaning: To put in full effort, to go for it,

no hesitation, no holding back.

Common where: Heard across Canada, especially in the West and North, and popular in outdoor sports, trades work, and anything involving snow, engines, or enthusiasm.

First heard: It became nationally recognizable in the

late 20th century as Canadians used it as a general encouragement.

The story: Whether you're shovelling the driveway, climbing a hill, or starting something ambitious, Canadians don't overthink it, they give'r. A simple word for maximum effort.

Homo Milk

Meaning: Short for homogenized milk. Usually the 3.25% whole milk found in Canadian grocery stores.

Common where: Used widely across Canada, especially on milk bags and cartons, store shelves, and in family kitchens.

First heard: The shorthand appeared in the mid-20th century alongside the rise of homogenization (the process that keeps the cream from separating).

The story: The term often surprises visitors who aren't used to the abbreviation, but Canadians barely notice it. To most households, homo milk simply means the red bag of whole milk in the dairy aisle.

Out for a Rip

Meaning: To head out for a quick drive, spin, or burst of fun, usually without a real destination.

Common where: Most often heard in Ontario and parts of the

Prairies, especially in smaller towns and rural areas.

First heard: Long used in local slang, it became widely known in 2013 after the viral comedy song "Out for a Rip" from a Kingston, Ontario rapper.

The story: Whether it's a car, a snowmobile, or anything with an engine, going "out for a rip" means blowing off steam and enjoying the ride, no plan required.

Bagged Milk

Meaning: Milk sold in a set of plastic pouches, usually three smaller bags tucked inside one larger outer sleeve. Each individual pouch is the milk bag you snip

open and drop into
the pitcher.

Common where: Most
common in Ontario
and parts of Atlantic
Canada. Less
common in Western
Canada and Quebec,
where cartons and
jugs are more typical.

First heard:
Introduced in the
1970s when Canada
switched to metric.
Bags adapted to the

new litre-based system more easily than plastic jugs, and the format stuck.

The story: It's second nature to Canadians: slide the bag into the pitcher, cut the corner, and pour. To visitors, the whole setup feels like a puzzle with too many pieces. Just another daily ritual that quietly marks life in parts of Canada.

Mountie

Meaning: A nickname for a member of the Royal Canadian Mounted Police (RCMP), Canada's federal police force.

Common where: Used across Canada in everyday conversation, tourism, media, and pop culture.

First heard: The term appeared in the early 1900s as a casual shorthand for the North-West Mounted Police, later the RCMP. It became widely recognized through books, newspapers, and early film.

The story: The red serge and Stetson hat made the Mountie one of Canada's most recognizable symbols. Whether solving cases or starring on postcards, the nickname stuck probably because it's friendly, familiar, and unmistakably Canadian.

The Great White North

Meaning: A playful nickname for Canada

that's part
geography, part
winter joke, and part
national pride.

Common where:
Heard across Canada
and often used in
media, tourism, and
comedy.

First heard:
Popularized in the
early 1980s by the
comedy duo Bob and
Doug McKenzie,
though references to

Canada as a northern, snow-covered country go back much further.

The story: Snow doesn't cover Canada year-round, but the nickname stuck anyway. It's a mix of humour and identity and the kind of self-aware, slightly exaggerated term Canadians enjoy using about themselves.

Thanks for Coming Along

From northern towns to downtown cafés, Canadians have been shaping their own way of speaking for generations. Some expressions are practical, others are funny, and many are simply part of everyday life across the country.

Thanks for coming along on this tour of familiar phrases. These pages show how language grows from ordinary moments and shared habits, whether it's a chat at the rink, a morning at the cottage, or a neighbourly interruption that starts with "Sorry, just one more thing."

About the Author

Jacqueline Cooper is a Canadian writer with a sharp eye for the offbeat details hiding in everyday life.

When she's not digging through statutes and bylaws for oddball trivia, she runs Little Goodbyes Press, a small indie

Canadian press creating books that mix humour, heart, and a dash of curiosity.

About the Publisher

Little Goodbyes Press is an independent Canadian publisher creating books that celebrate curious details, gentle humour, and unexpected stories.

From children's picture books to quirky trivia, every

title is made with care and just enough Canadian flavour to make you smile.

Looking for more books? Be sure to visit us on our website at: www.littlegoodbyes.ca